# Learning About My Body

Young learners need to know that scientists are not just workers wearing white jackets in laboratories. We do science when we

- cook breakfast
- mix paints to make new colors
- plant seeds in the garden
- watch a squirrel in a tree
- mark how tall we are on a growth chart, or
- look outside to see what the weather is like

The activities in this book relate to the National Science Education Standards (Science as Inquiry). When you follow the step-by-step lessons, your students will be doing science. They will

- observe
- predict
- compare
- order
- categorize

- ask meaningful questions
- conduct investigations
- record information
- communicate investigations and explanations
- use tools and equipment

What makes this book easy for you?

- The step-by-step activities are easy to understand and include illustrations where it's important.

- The resources you need are at your fingertips: record sheets; logbook sheets; and other reproducibles such as minibooks, task cards, and picture cards.

- Each science concept is presented in a self-contained section. You can decide to do the entire book or pick only those sections that enhance your own curriculum.

*minibooks*

*task cards*

*logbooks*

*picture cards*

# Using Logbooks as Learning Tools

*ScienceWorks for Kids* emphasizes the use of logbooks to help students summarize and solidify learning.

Logbooks are valuable learning tools for several reasons:

• Logbooks give students an opportunity to put what they are learning into their own words.

• Putting ideas into words is an important step in internalizing new information. Whether spoken or written, this experience allows students to synthesize their thinking.

• Explaining and describing experiences helps students make connections between several concepts and ideas.

• Logbook entries allow the teacher to catch misunderstandings right away and then reteach.

• Logbooks are a useful reference for students and a record of what has been learned.

## Two Types of Logbooks

This picture stands for class logbook

Throughout the unit, a class logbook will be used to record student understanding.

• Use large sheets of chart paper.

• Hold the pages together with metal rings.

Even though your students may not be reading, the responses can be read to them as a means of confirming and reviewing learning.

This picture stands for student logbook

page 3

My Body Logbook

Name:

Students process their understanding of investigations by writing or drawing their responses in individual student logbooks. Following the investigations are record and activity sheets that can be added to each student's logbook.

At the conclusion of the unit, reproduce a copy of the logbook cover on page 3 for each student. Students organize their pages and staple them with the cover.

My Body
Logbook

Name:

Learning About My Body • EMC 869

# Teacher Preparation

Before beginning this unit on the human body, make the following preparations.

- Collect: stethoscope, model skeleton, x-rays (optional)

- Invite a dentist or dental hygienist to visit the class to discuss good dental care.

- Prepare the human body puzzle on pages 78–80.

  Reproduce the body part patterns. Glue them to tagboard. Add Velcro® or magnetic tape to use the patterns on a flannel board or magnetic board. (You will need to put Velcro® or magnetic tape on both sides of the exterior puzzle pieces in order to place the skeleton or internal organs on the body.)

  Place the puzzle in a center for independent practice.

- Gather an assortment of books about the human body, how it works, and how to care for it. (See the inside back cover for a bibliography to use throughout the study of the human body.)

  Also available from Evan-Moor: *The Human Body*—EMC 863. This set contains full-color pictures of the human body systems, plus a set of life cycle sequencing cards. The back of each card contains information about the part or system.

pages 78–80

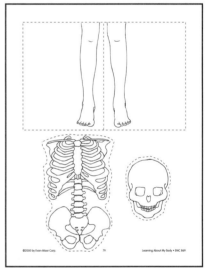

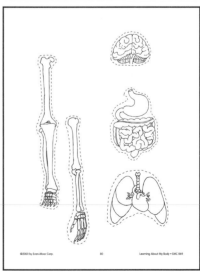

I found my collarbone!

My Amazing Body

# The body has external parts.

## My Body

- Ask a child to stand in front of the class. Ask, "When you look at (child's name) what do you see?" Allow time for students to describe the child. Then say, "You said (child) is tall and has brown hair and blue eyes. You said he has two arms and two legs. What are all the things you named a part of?" Question students until you get the answer *his/her body*.

Begin the class logbook by listing the parts of the body named by students on a sheet of chart paper. Answers will depend on students' prior knowledge. Don't list information not offered by students. Add details as your students acquire more information.

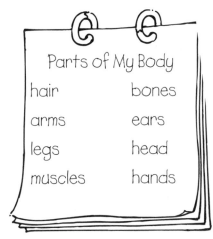

### Parts of My Body

| | |
|---|---|
| hair | bones |
| arms | ears |
| legs | head |
| muscles | hands |

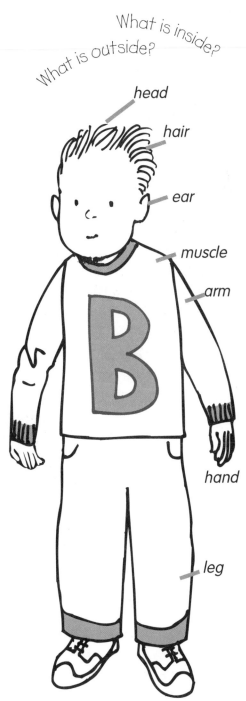

What is outside?    What is inside?

head
hair
ear
muscle
arm
hand
leg

Go back through the list and ask students to decide if a part is on the outside or inside of the body. Circle the external body parts.

- Read *My Body, Your Body* by Mick Manning and appropriate parts of *The Human Body: A First Discovery Book* by Sylvaine Perols (see bibliography on the inside back cover) to share more general information about the human body. Add new ideas to the class logbook.

## The Outside Parts

Use the following activities to develop vocabulary for naming external parts of the body.

> Basic—back, chin, hip, thumb, chest, elbow, shoulder, waist, ankle, etc.

> Advanced—calf, earlobe, sole, palm, thigh, wrist, knuckles, armpit, etc.

page 78

- Play "Show Me." Teacher names a body part. Students point to it on their own body and repeat the name.

- Use the exterior body pieces of the human body puzzle on pages 78 and 79. Put it together on a flannel board. Name the various parts of the body and locate them on the puzzle.

- Working with a partner, students are to name the various external body parts shown on the form on page 8. They then color the picture and place it in their logbooks.

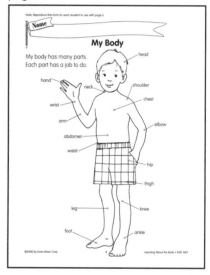

page 8

## How Is It Used?

- Explain that each part of the human body can do one or more jobs for us. Read *Here Are My Hands* by Bill Martin, Jr., & John Archambault; *How Do We Move?* by Carol Ballard; or *I Can Move* by Mandy Suhr to find some of the ways the body parts are used.

- Discuss and demonstrate the different types of movements the body can make. Include small movements such as nodding, turning the head, or blinking as well as whole body movements such as hopping and skipping. Name the body part or parts involved in the movement.

- Ask students to create riddles about their body parts. Model the activity and then call on students to ask their own riddles.

> *I am the part of your body that can kick a ball. What am I?*
>
> *I am the part between your head and your shoulders. What am I?*
>
> *I am the part of your body that can smell pizza. What am I?*

- Make "Children in Action" following the instructions on page 7. Pin the completed pictures on a bulletin board.

# Children in Action

## Materials

- pattern on page 9, reproduced for each student
- 12" x 18" (30.5 x 45.5 cm) piece of construction paper
- scissors
- crayons
- paste

## Steps to Follow

Model how to move the pieces around to show different movements. Then have students follow these steps:

1. Color and cut out the pieces.

2. Lay them on the construction paper to form a body.

3. Move the pieces around to create a body in action. Paste the pieces to the construction paper.

4. Use crayons to add details.

5. Students write or dictate a phrase or sentence about what the body is doing and what body parts are being used.

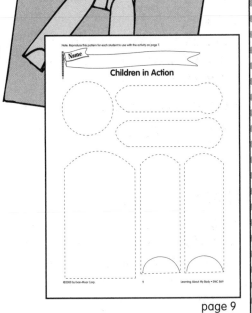

page 9

## Making Connections—More Alike Than Different

- Compare how people look alike and different, using photographs, pictures from magazines, or students in the class.

- Make a large masking tape circle on the playground. Have students stand outside the circle. Describe a physical feature (brown eyes, one nose, etc.). Everyone in class with that feature steps into the circle. Continue naming characteristics, with students moving in and out of the circle. Occasionally name a characteristic that none of the children possess (three arms). End with a feature that is the same for all students in your class.

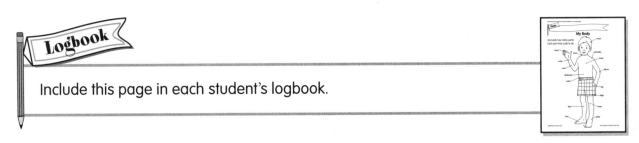

Logbook

Include this page in each student's logbook.

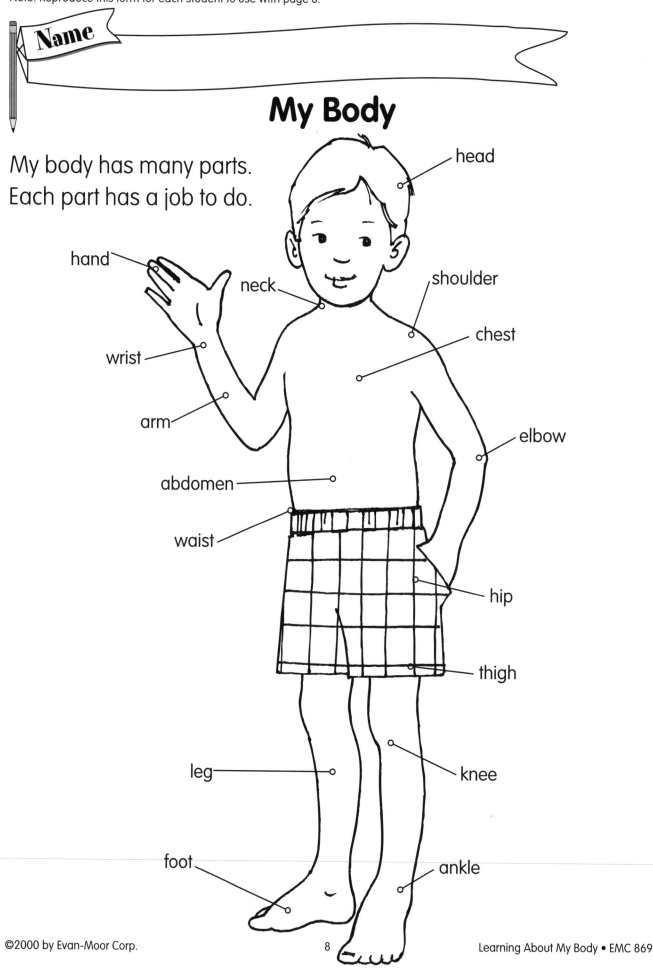

# My Body

Name

My body has many parts.
Each part has a job to do.

head

hand

neck

shoulder

chest

wrist

arm

elbow

abdomen

waist

hip

thigh

leg

knee

foot

ankle

8

Name

# Children in Action

9

# The body has internal parts— skeleton and muscles.

## The Inside Parts

- Review the body parts charted previously. Ask students to recall which were parts found inside a human body. *(We have a heart. I have bones inside my body.)*

- Read appropriate parts of *Me and My Amazing Body* by Joan Sweeney to explore the "insides" of the human body.

## I Have a Skeleton

- Remind students that they said we have bones inside our bodies. Ask, "What are all the bones together called?" *(skeleton)* Read and discuss *Bones* by Anna Sandeman.

- Begin a chart entitled "Inside My Body." As each part is studied, students will name the internal part and tell what it does for the body.

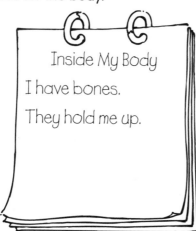

Inside My Body

I have bones.

They hold me up.

- Borrow x-rays to share with students so they can see various types of bones. Or bring in a model of a human skeleton for students to study.

- Have students try to feel their own bones. See if they can count their ribs.

- Use the body puzzle on pages 78–80. Call on students to place the bones in the correct places on the exterior body pieces. Then have each student put together the skeleton on pages 12 and 13.

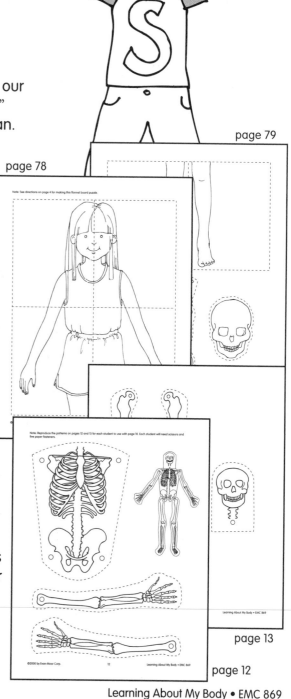

page 79

page 78

page 13

page 12

- Students complete pages 14 and 15 for their logbooks. Using page 14, they match bones to the correct body parts. Using page 15, they paste the pieces in order to show the ribs protecting the heart and lungs. Students draw their own face on the body.

## I Have Muscles

- Discuss the purpose of muscles in the body. Use questioning to help students reach an understanding that muscles are necessary to move the bones of the body.

- Add *muscles* to the "Inside My Body" chart and ask students to describe what muscles can do.

- Students feel their muscles. Say, "Put your hands on your cheeks. Now smile. Can you feel your muscles working? Now show me how big you can make the muscle in your arm. Pull the muscles across your abdomen tight. Can you feel how they change?"

- Using page 16, help students locate the muscles and color them.

page 14

page 15

page 16

I can feel my muscles move when I smile.

Logbook

Include these pages in each student's logbook.

Note: Reproduce the patterns on pages 12 and 13 for each student to use with page 10. Each student will need scissors and five paper fasteners.

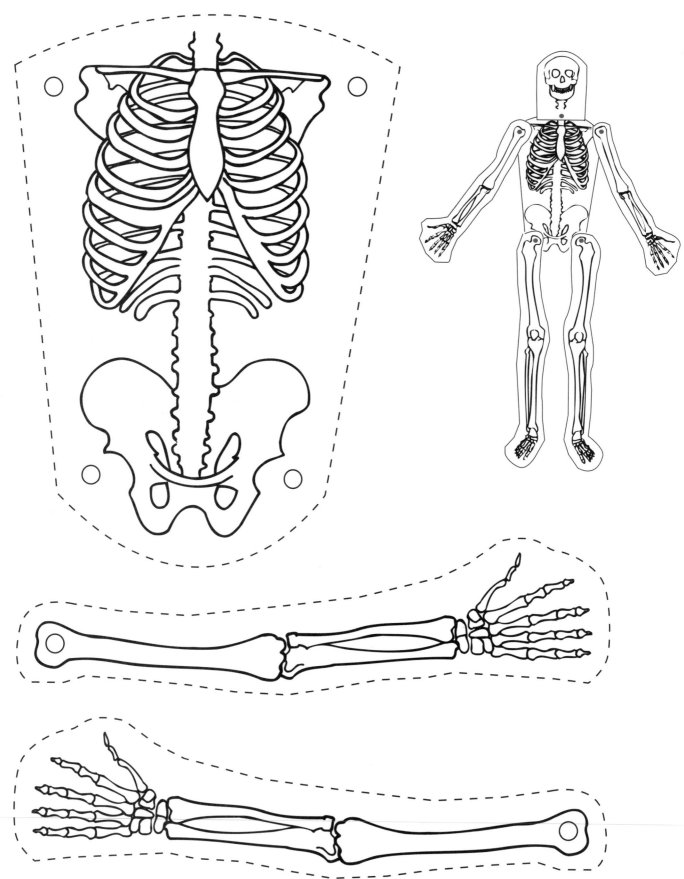

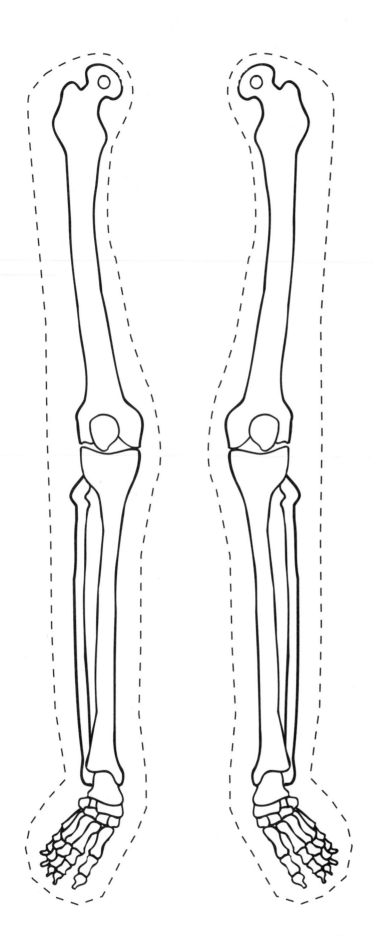

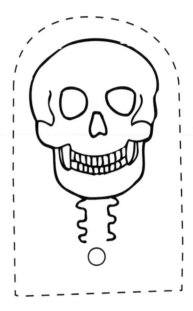

Learning About My Body • EMC 869

**Name**

# Where Are the Bones?

Match.

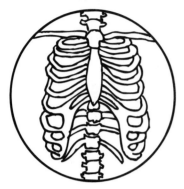

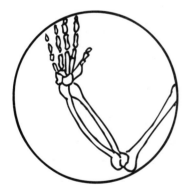

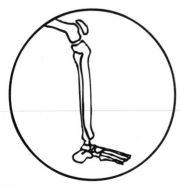

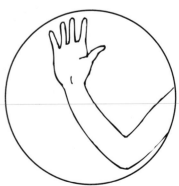

Note: Reproduce this form for each student to use with page 11.

**Name**

# My Skeleton

My rib cage protects my heart and lungs.

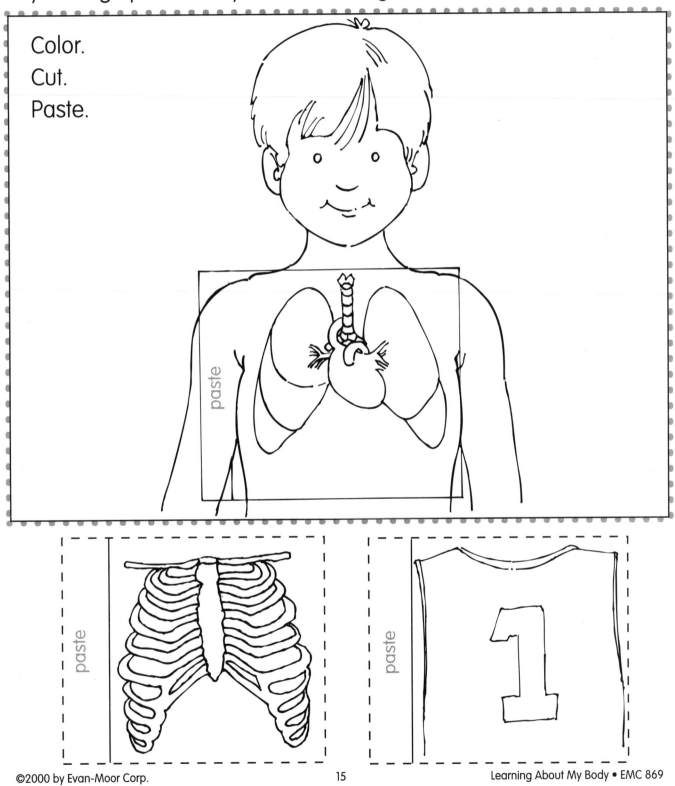

Color.
Cut.
Paste.

paste

paste

paste

Learning About My Body • EMC 869

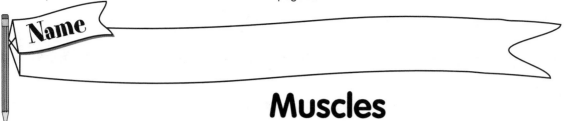

# Muscles

My muscles help move my body.

Color the muscles.

# The body has internal parts– heart and lungs.

## I Have a Heart

- Explain that there are some special muscles in the body. One of these special muscles is the heart. Discuss the job of the heart. Help students understand that the heart pumps blood around the body through little tubes. The blood takes oxygen and food to all the parts of the body. (Don't expect students to remember all of this information. You are setting the groundwork for greater understanding when they are older.)

- Add *heart* to the "Inside My Body" chart and ask students to describe what the heart does for the body.

- Have students look at the veins in their wrists and hands. Explain that these are some of the little tubes that carry the blood back to their hearts after the oxygen is used up.

- Use a stethoscope so students can hear their hearts beat.

- Using page 19, students color the heart.

## I Have Lungs

- Have students hold their rib cages as they breathe in and out so they can feel their chest getting larger and smaller. Ask students to explain what is happening. Use questioning to help them explain that air is going in and out of their bodies. Ask them to name the part of the body that is being used. Name *lungs* if no one can provide an answer.

- Read and discuss *Breathing* by Anna Sandeman.

- Add *lungs* to the "Inside My Body" chart, asking students to describe what the lungs do for the body.

- Have students breathe in and out, trying to feel the movement of the air. Explain that the nose cleans and warms the air as they breathe. Do the experiment on page 18 to discover how much air their lungs can hold.

- Using page 20, students label the lungs breathing in and the lungs breathing out.

page 19

page 20

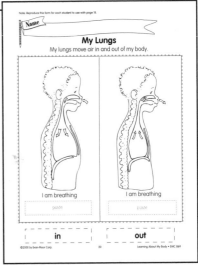

## My Lungs Hold Air

### Materials

- pan
- clean jar
- bendable drinking straw
- card large enough to cover the jar opening
- water

### Steps to Follow

1. Fill the pan half full of water.

2. Fill the jar with water. Hold a card on the mouth of the filled jar and turn it upside down into the pan of water.

3. Tilt the jar slightly so you can put the end of a curved straw under the jar's edge.

4. Blow one time into the straw. Blow out as much air as you can in one try to see how much air was in your lungs.

 **Logbook**

Include these pages in each student's logbook.

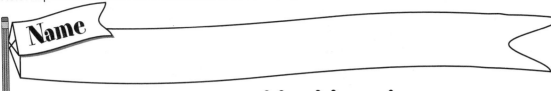
Name

# My Heart

My heart pumps blood around my body.

Color the heart.

Name

# My Lungs

My lungs move air in and out of my body.

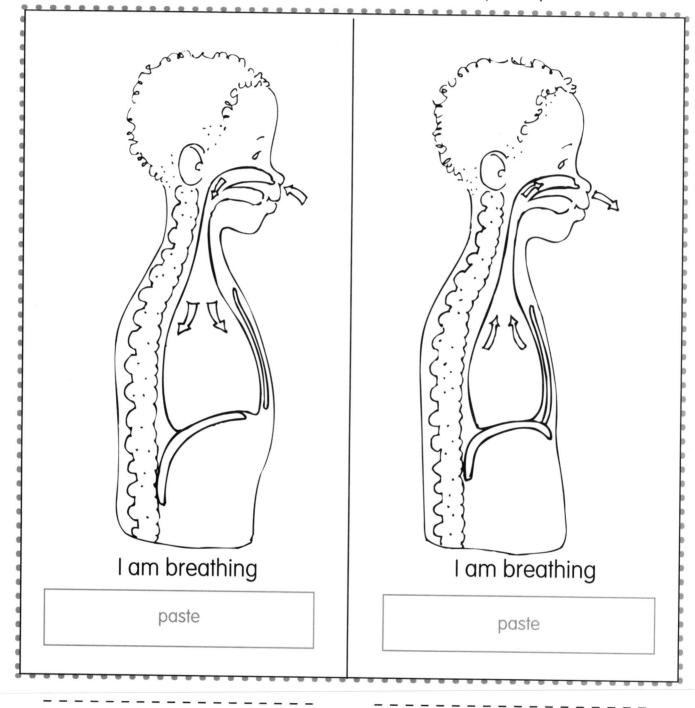

I am breathing

paste

I am breathing

paste

in

out

20

# The body has internal parts—stomach and intestines.

## I Have a Stomach and Intestines

- Have students chew on pieces of apple to see how their teeth make them small enough to swallow. Have students feel their throat as they swallow the bits of apple. Ask, "Where is the food going when you swallow?" Provide *stomach* if they are unable to give an answer.

- Read and discuss *Eating* by Anna Sandeman and/or *What Happens to a Hamburger* by Paul Showers to learn more about what happens to the food we eat.

- Add *stomach* and *intestines* to the "Inside My Body" chart and ask students to describe what they do for the body.

- Bring a blender to school. Blend bits of apple with a little water to show how the stomach turns the apple into a soupy mixture. Explain that when the apple is in small enough bits, it can be taken to all parts of the body.

- Using page 22, students trace the path of a piece of apple through the digestive system.

page 22

page 26

## Inside My Body

- Using the minibook on pages 23–25, review the internal body parts and their functions.

- Use the internal body pieces of the human body puzzle on page 80. Add the internal organs to the correct places on the exterior body pieces.

- Using page 26, students paste internal body parts in the correct locations.

Include these pages in each student's logbook.

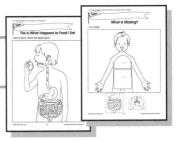

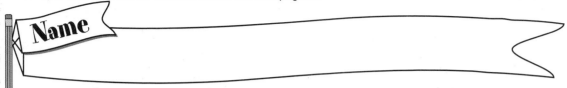

Name

# This Is What Happens to Food I Eat

Color to show where the apple goes.

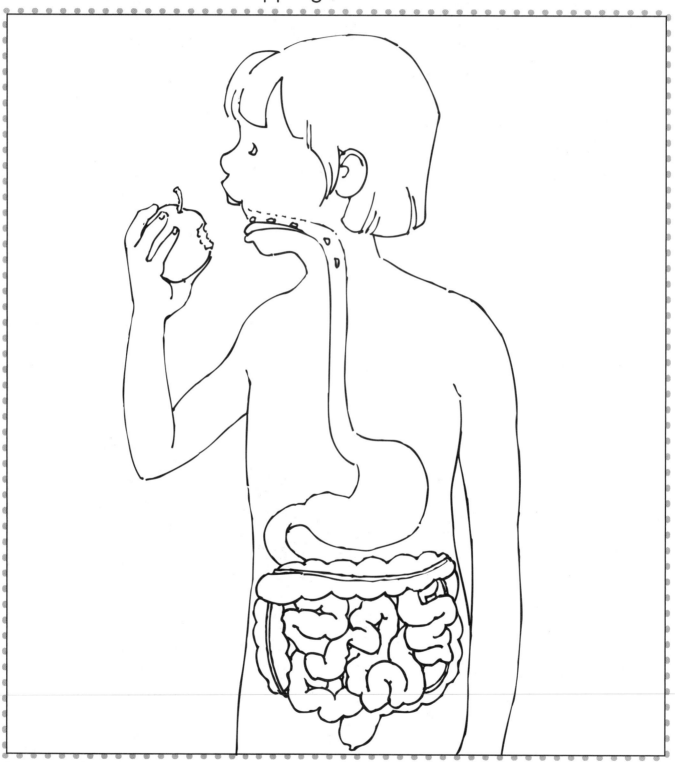

# Inside My Body

Name:

1

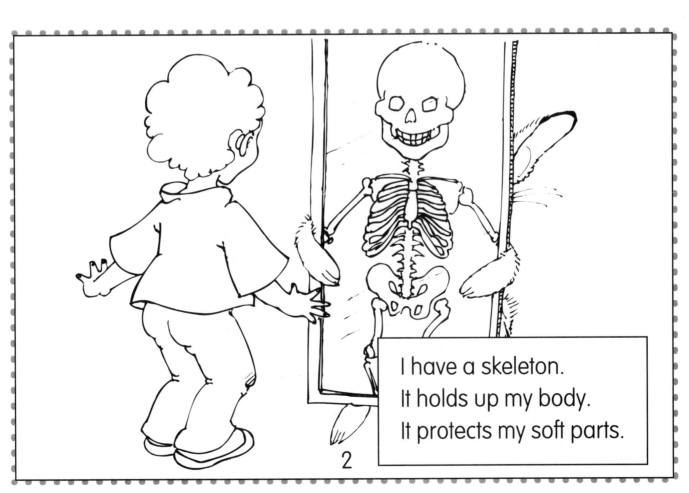

I have a skeleton.
It holds up my body.
It protects my soft parts.

2

I have muscles.
They move my bones when I walk or run.
They help me smile and scratch my nose.

3

Learning About My Body • EMC 869

I have a heart.
It pumps blood around my body.
My blood takes food and oxygen to every part.

4

I have a stomach and intestines.
I get energy from the food I eat.
My stomach and intestines digest
the food so I can use its energy.

5

Learning About My Body • EMC 869

I have lungs.
I breathe in air.
My lungs get
oxygen from the air.

6

Name

# What Is Missing?

Cut. Paste.

paste

paste

# The brain controls body functions and is the center of thinking.

## The Brain

- Ask students to think about how their bodies know what to do. "How do your legs and feet know when to move? How do you know when it is cold or hot?" Use questioning to help students identify the functions of the brain (thinking, emotions, movement, speech, sight, hearing, etc.). Provide examples of the various functions named.

- Reproduce page 28 for each student. Fold as indicated. Read and discuss the information.

- Complete a chart entitled "My Brain" explaining what the brain does for the body.

- Read and discuss *Brain* by Anna Sandeman and/or appropriate parts of *How Do We Think?* by Carol Ballard or *Look Inside Your Brain* by Heather Alexander. Add new information to the chart.

## The Skull

- Explain that the brain is soft, so it needs to be protected. If the brain is injured, a person will not be able to do many of the things he or she could do before. Ask, "How does your body protect your brain?" Guide students to name the skull.

- Ask, "What can you do to protect your brain?" Guide students to name such things as using seat belts and wearing safety helmets when riding bikes, skating, etc.

- Have students illustrate one way they can protect their brain. Place the completed drawings in the students' logbooks.

- Using the worksheet on page 29, students color, cut out, and paste the pieces in order to show the skull protecting the brain. Have them draw their own face on the top piece. Have students glue the completed project to a sheet of 8.5" x 11" (21 x 28 cm) paper and place it in their logbooks.

page 28

page 29

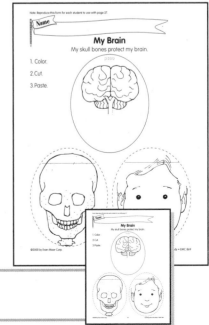

Include this page in each student's logbook.

Learning About My Body • EMC 869

Inside my head is my brain.

1

**My Brain**

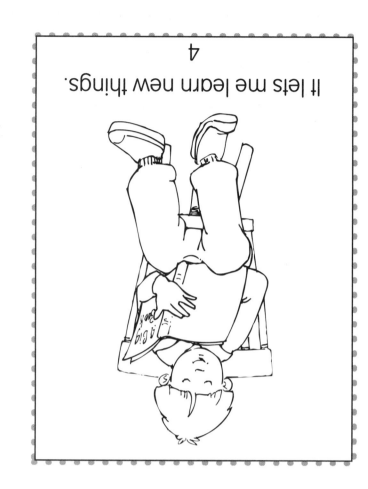

It lets me learn new things.

4

It tells my body when to move.

2

It tells my body what to do.

3

Time to get up!

Name

# My Brain
## My skull bones protect my brain.

1. Color.

2. Cut.

3. Paste.

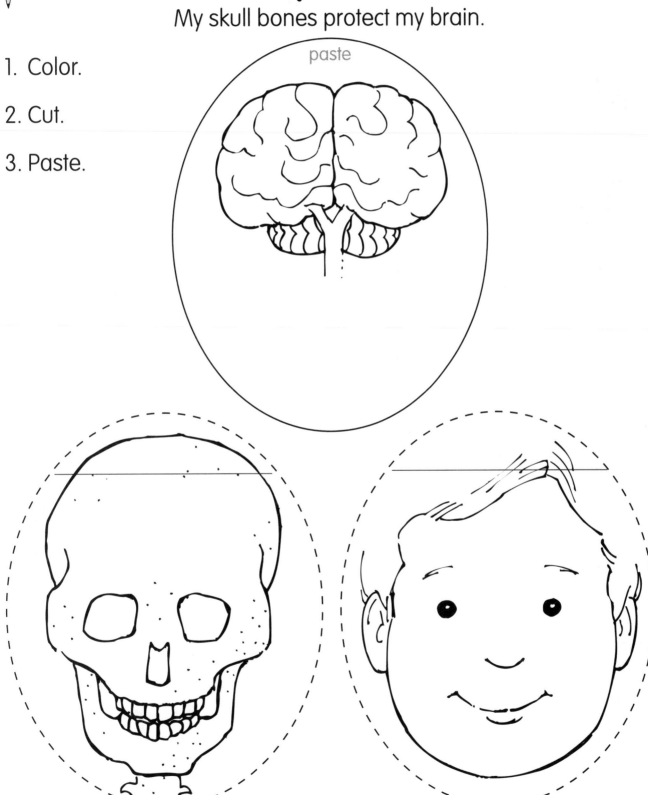

paste

29
Learning About My Body • EMC 869

# Humans use their five senses to find out about their surroundings.

*Note: Each of the five senses is covered in greater detail in the following chapters.*

## My Five Senses

- Read *My Five Senses* by Aliki or *Senses* by Anna Sandeman. Ask students to recall the names of the senses and how they are used.

- Record student responses on a chart entitled "My Five Senses."

My Five Senses
They help me.
I hear with my ears.

Sight

Hearing

Smell

Taste

Touch

- Ask a riddle that requires students to identify either the sense being used or the part of the body that provides that sense.

  "I hear with this part of my body." *(ears)*

  "I use my tongue to do this." *(taste things)*

  After doing several examples, have students make up their own riddles.

- Read appropriate parts of *My Brain and Senses* by Paul Bennett. Review the names of the senses. Ask students to name the parts of their body that have those functions. Add this information to the class log.

# Hearing

## My Sense of Hearing

- Read *The Listening Walk* by Paul Showers. Discuss what the characters heard on their walk. Then take students on a "listening walk." When you return to the class, share what was heard.

- List the sounds on a chart entitled "Hearing." Talk about which sounds were from nature and which were manmade.

- Using the form on page 32 and drawing paper cut into the same shape, students illustrate one thing they heard on the walk. Staple illustrations together in a book entitled "We Hear Sounds."

- Bring in a collection of objects that make sounds. Students close their eyes and try to identify each object by the sound.

- Conduct the "Match the Sounds" activity below.

- Make a sound tape. Include common sounds (e.g., door closing) and not-so-common sounds (e.g., pencil being sharpened). Play the tape and ask students to guess what is making each sound.

- Using page 33, students color the items that can be heard. Using page 34, students draw or write five sounds they can hear right now.

Hearing
birds singing
car horns
barking dogs

We Hear Sounds

## Match the Sounds

This may be done as a small-group activity or by an individual at a learning center.

### Materials

- blindfold
- 12 small jars with lids (Fill two jars half full with each of the items.)
- pebbles
- marbles
- rice
- cotton balls
- beans
- paper clips

### Steps to Follow

Put on the blindfold. Shake the jars. Find two that sound alike. Match up all the jars, then take off the blindfold and check yourself.

Include these pages in each student's logbook.

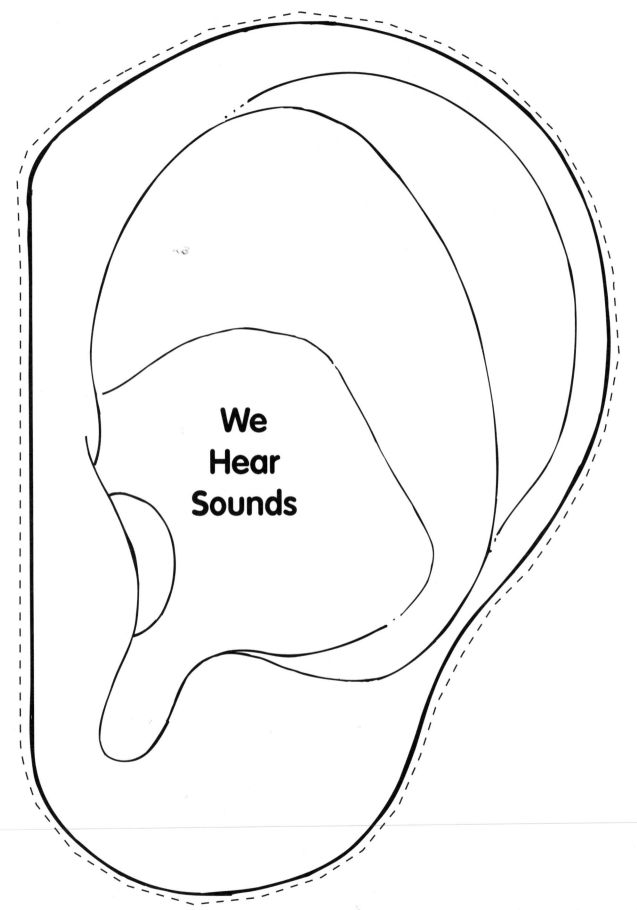

We
Hear
Sounds

**Name**

# What Can You Hear?

Color the things that make a sound.

I hear with my _____.

33  Learning About My Body • EMC 869

Name

# What Can You Hear?

Draw or list five sounds you can hear right now.

Learning About My Body • EMC 869

# Sight

## My Sense of Sight

- Discuss the ways the things we see can be described (color, size, etc.). Then go outside to play "I Spy."

- Read *The Eye Book* by Dr. Seuss. Then take students on a "seeing walk." (Look for specific categories of things—color, size, use, etc.) When you return to class, share what was seen.

- List objects seen on the seeing walk on a chart entitled "Seeing." Sort the objects into natural objects and manmade objects.

- Using the form on page 36 and paper cut in the same shape, students illustrate one thing they saw on the walk. Staple these together to form a shape book entitled "What We Saw."

## Exploring Sight

- Let students peek at a tray containing three or more items. (The number will depend on the age and ability of your students.) Name each item with your students. Have everyone close their eyes or turn their backs as you remove one item. Students turn back and try to decide what is missing. You can make the task more difficult by mixing up the items or by removing two items at one time.

- Using page 37, students draw or list five things they can see right now.

page 37

Note: Reproduce this pattern for each student to use with page 35.

What We Saw

Note: Reproduce this form for each student to use with page 35.

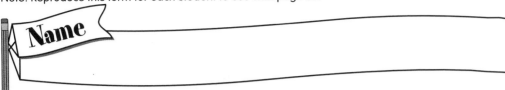

**Name**

# What Do You See?

Draw or list five things you can see right now.

I see with my _____.

     Learning About My Body • EMC 869

# Smell

page 40

## My Sense of Smell

- Discuss how smells can be described. Have students give examples of "good" smells and "bad" smells. Then take students on a "smelling walk." Sniff out good and not-so-good smells.

- List the objects that give off the smells on a chart entitled "Smelling." Sort the objects into natural smells and manmade smells.

- Using the form on page 39 and paper cut in the same shape, students illustrate one pleasant smell from the walk. Staple these together to form a shape book entitled "Our Favorite Smells."

page 41

## Exploring Smell

- Conduct the "Match the Smells" activity below.

- Using page 40, students circle things that smell good and cross out things that smell bad. Using page 41, students draw something they like to smell and something they don't like to smell.

---

## Match the Smells

This may be done as a small-group activity or by an individual in a learning center.

### Materials

- blindfold
- 12 small jars with lids
- 12 cotton balls
- lemon juice
- pickle juice
- perfume
- vanilla extract
- ground nutmeg
- ground cinnamon

Apply each substance to two cotton balls. Place one cotton ball in each jar. Put on the lids. Mix up the jars.

### Steps to Follow

Put on the blindfold. Open one jar at a time. Find two that smell alike. Match up all the jars, then take off the blindfold and check yourself.

Include these pages in each student's logbook.

Note: Reproduce this pattern for each student to use with page 38.

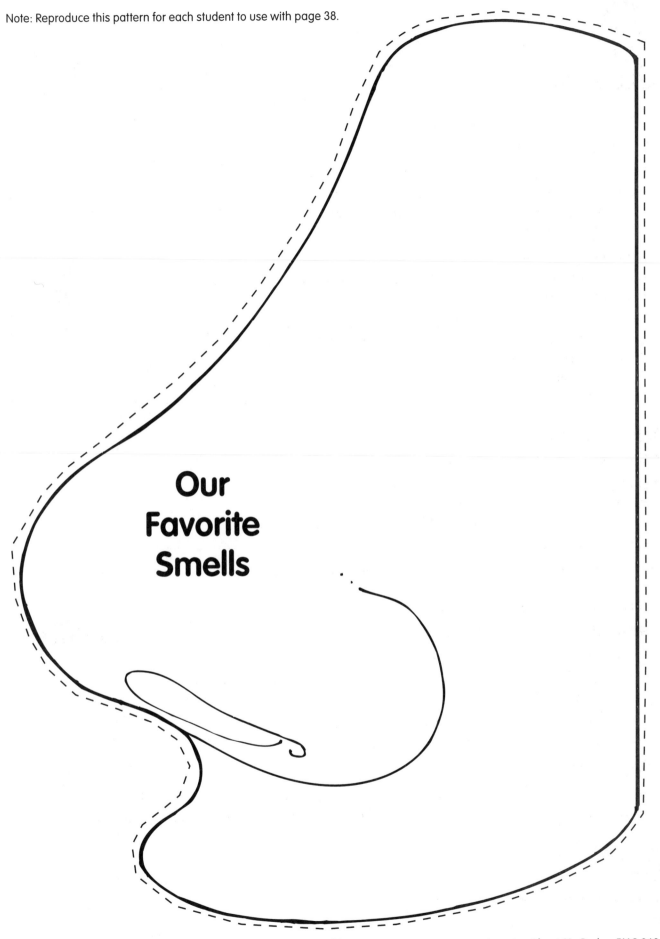

## Our
## Favorite
## Smells

Learning About My Body • EMC 869

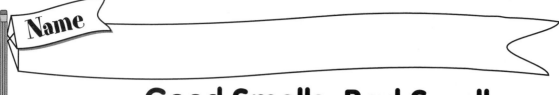
Name

# Good Smells, Bad Smells

Circle the things that smell good.

Make an **X** on the things that smell bad.

I smell with my _____.

Learning About My Body • EMC 869

Name

# Good Smells, Bad Smells

Draw something you like to smell.

Draw something you don't like to smell.

# Taste

## My Sense of Taste

- Read and discuss *Taste* by Maria Rius. Then, using the form on page 43, students illustrate a taste they like. Staple these together to form a shape book entitled "Tasty Treats."

- Ask students to describe how they use their sense of taste. Record their responses on a chart entitled "Tasting."

## Exploring Taste

- Have a tasting time. Include salty, sweet, and sour foods. Ask students to taste small bites and describe the tastes.

   **Note:** *It is important to consider any food allergies students may have when selecting foods for tasting.*

- Play "What Do You Taste?" It is harder to recognize the taste of food if you cannot see it. Put pieces of apple, raw potato, and carrot on small plates. Have students work in pairs. One student closes his or her eyes. The other student carefully feeds a food to his or her partner. The partner guesses what the food is. Reverse roles and repeat the "tasting."

- Using page 44, students match items that have similar tastes (sweet, sour, salty).

Tasting

We put food in our mouth.

It can taste good.

It can taste bad.

page 44

That tastes like an orange.

Logbook

Include this page in each student's logbook.

Note: Reproduce this pattern for each student to use with page 42.

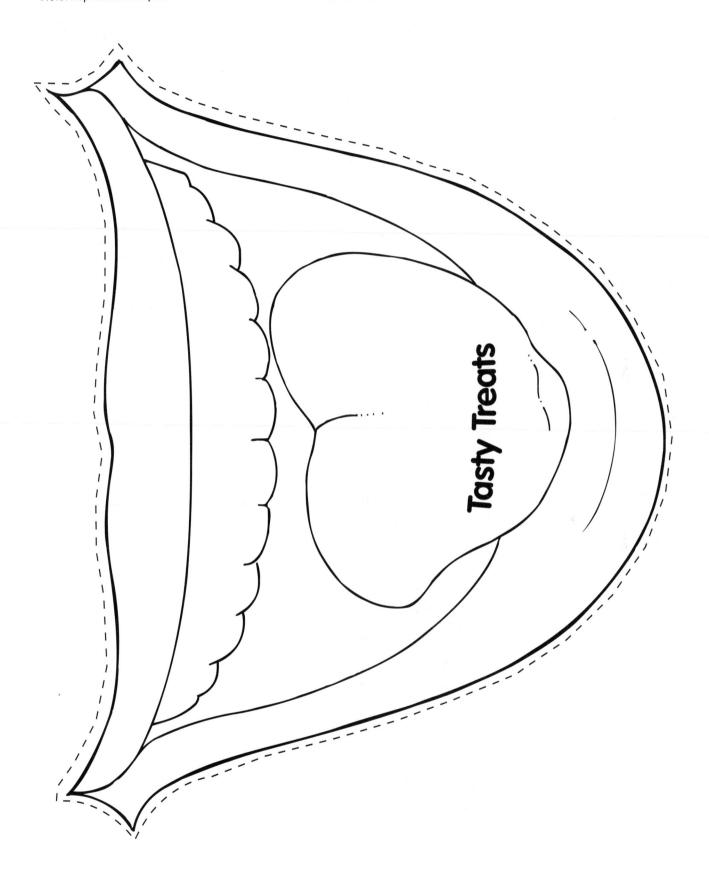

Tasty Treats

43

Note: Reproduce this form for each student to use with page 42.

## Tastes

Match.

I like the taste of _____.

I taste with my

Learning About My Body • EMC 869

# Touch

## My Sense of Touch

- Have students sit in a circle. Pass around objects with different textures (smooth block, sandpaper, velvet cloth, beanbag, ice cube, plastic cup, rough rock, etc.). As students describe what they are feeling, begin a list of descriptive words on chart paper or the chalkboard (*smooth, rough, soft, hard, cold, warm, sharp, scratchy, fluffy, squishy, bumpy, slick, etc.*).

- Take students on a "touching walk." (This is a good time to discuss what can be touched and what shouldn't be touched.) When you return to class, share the different textures that were felt. Ask students to describe how something felt and why it felt that way. *(The tree felt rough. It had bumps and cracks on it.)*

- List objects felt on the walk on a chart entitled "Touching." Add a descriptive word to each item on the list.

- Have each student bring in one object with an interesting texture (bark, piece of cloth, sandpaper, etc.). Using the form on page 46, students attach their object and write a phrase or sentence that describes how it feels. Staple these together to form a shape book entitled "Touch This."

Touching

We touch to feel things.
bark—rough, hard
rock—heavy, bumpy
grass—soft, smooth

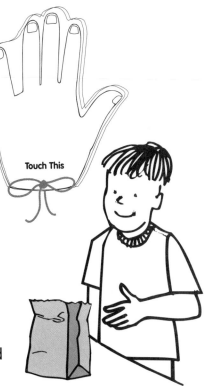

**Touch This**

## Exploring Touch

- Prepare several "Mystery Bags" by placing one item in each small bag. Select a student to use only his or her sense of touch to try to identify the object. Have the student describe the item aloud as he or she tries to name it. If the first student can't name the item, call on a second student to try. Show the item to verify the answer.

- Using page 47, students color the items that can safely be touched and cross out objects that shouldn't be touched. Using page 48, students review all five senses.

Include these pages in each student's logbook.

          Learning About My Body • EMC 869

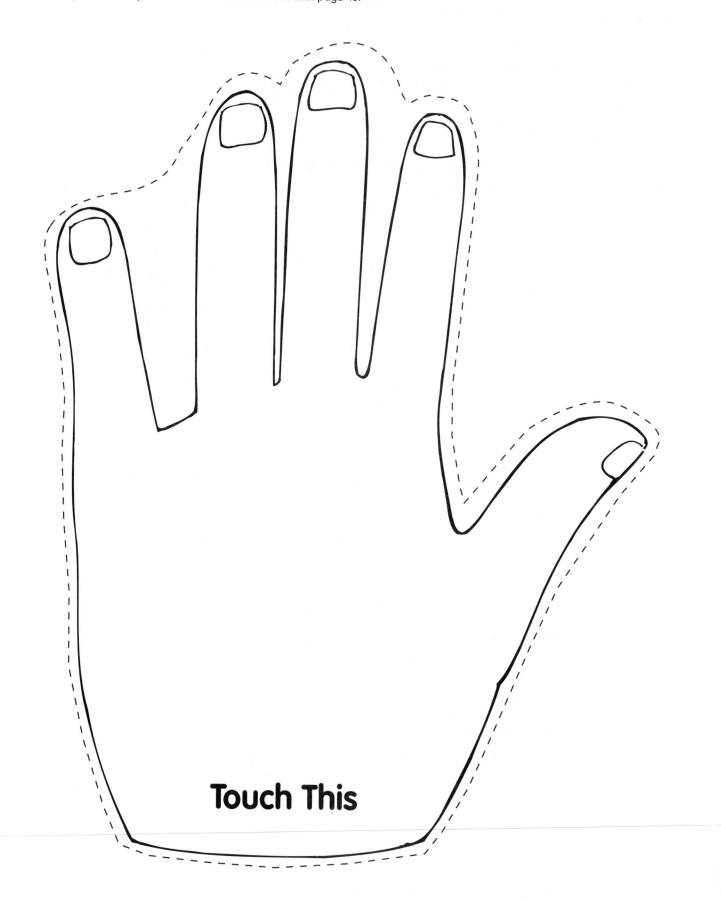

**Touch This**

**Name**

# Do Not Touch!

Color the things you can touch.

Make an **X** on the things you should **not** touch.

I feel with my

I feel with other parts of my skin, too.

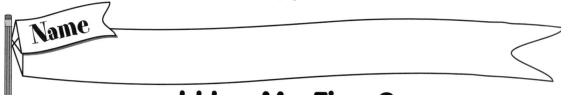
**Name**

# I Use My Five Senses

Circle the senses you use.

# Humans grow and change during their life cycle.

## We Change As We Grow

- Collect pictures of school personnel (teacher, principal, librarian, etc.) both as babies and as adults. See if students can correctly match the pictures. Ask "How has _____ changed since he (or she) was a baby?"

  Encourage students to describe the ways they have changed themselves since they were babies.

- Have students bring in pictures of themselves as babies. Post these pictures with their current pictures so they can see the physical changes that have occurred.

- Complete a chart entitled "How We Change."

How We Change
We get bigger.
We look different.

## Watch Us Grow

- Everybody grows at a different rate. Using adding machine tape, measure students. Pin the strips to a large bulletin board to make a height graph.

  In a few months, measure students again. This time use a strip of red roving. Pin the roving onto the adding machine tape to show how much they have grown.

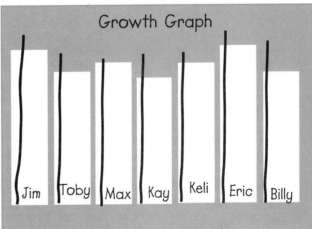

Growth Graph

Jim   Toby   Max   Kay   Keli   Eric   Billy

- Give each student a 12″ x 24″ (30.5 x 61 cm) sheet of butcher paper folded into thirds. Students cut out the phrases on page 51, glue one phrase in each section, and draw a picture of themselves at each life stage.

- Using pages 52 and 53, students sequence the human life cycle.

page 52

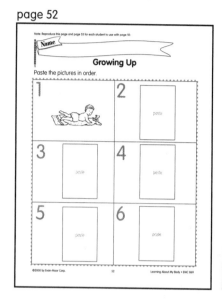

page 53

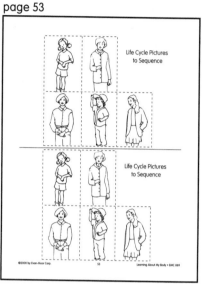

## Making Connections

Explain that other living things also change as they grow. Ask students to think of the ways an animal changes as it grows. Then ask them to think of ways in which a plant changes.

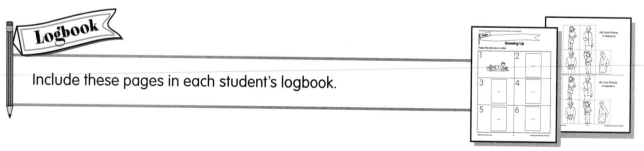

Include these pages in each student's logbook.

Note: Reproduce these phrases for each student to use with page 50.

| | |
|---|---|
| as a baby | as a baby |
| now | now |
| grown up | grown up |
| as a baby | as a baby |
| now | now |
| grown up | grown up |
| as a baby | as a baby |
| now | now |
| grown up | grown up |
| as a baby | as a baby |
| now | now |
| grown up | grown up |

Name

# Growing Up

Paste the pictures in order.

| 1 | 2 |
|---|---|
| | paste |
| **3** | **4** |
| paste | paste |
| **5** | **6** |
| paste | paste |

Life Cycle Pictures
to Sequence

Life Cycle Pictures
to Sequence

# Nutrition

## Taking Care of My Body

- Ask students to explain why they need to take care of their bodies.

  *So I can grow big.*
  *I need to be strong.*
  *You can get sick if you don't.*

  Then have students come up with suggestions for how to take care of their bodies.

- List student ideas on a chart entitled "I Take Care of My Body." Have students illustrate the ideas listed. Attach a picture by each item listed on the chart.

  Explain that they will be learning more about ways to care for their bodies.

I Take Care of My Body
I eat good food.
I drink milk.
I wash my hands.

## I Eat Healthy Foods

- Say, "You said one of the ways we can take care of our bodies is to eat good food. Why do we need to eat food?" *(for energy; to grow hair, skin, muscles, and bones; to stay well)* "Let's name some foods that will help us stay healthy and grow." Ask students to explain their choices.

  Explain that some foods taste good but are not good for us if we eat too much of them. Ask students to name some of these foods. Remind students that it is all right to eat these foods sometimes, but that the other foods are healthier for us.

I Eat Healthy Foods

Name:

- Read and discuss the minibook on pages 56–58.

- List foods that are good for the body on a chart entitled "Healthy Foods."

- Divide students into small groups. Give each group several magazines and/or newspaper ads containing food items. Each group is to find several pictures showing foods that help us stay healthy and grow strong and one that does not. Provide time for groups to share their choices with the class.

## Healthy Snacks

Have a "healthy snack" tasting day. Provide a variety of fruits, vegetables, etc., for students to sample. Include snacks representative of various ethnic groups. (This is a good time to call on parent volunteers both to provide snacks and to assist in serving them.)

**Note:** *When you select snacks to share, be aware of any food allergies your students might have.*

## Pack a Healthy Lunch

Give each student a brown lunch bag. Discuss what kinds of food could be a part of a healthy lunch. Students draw healthy lunch items (or cut out magazine pictures). Then they paste the "lunch" on their bag.

# I Eat Healthy Foods

Name:

1

Your body is like a car.
A car needs fuel to go.
Your body needs fuel, too.

If you put the wrong fuel in your car, it won't work well.
If you put the wrong fuel in your body, it won't work well either.

2

I eat fruits and vegetables.

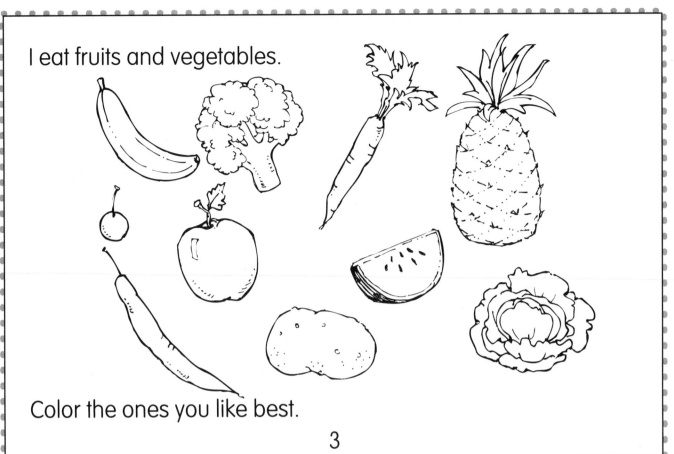

Color the ones you like best.

3

Learning About My Body • EMC 869

I drink milk and eat dairy products.

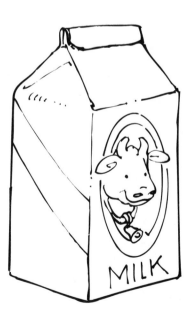

Make an **X** on the ones you like best.

4

I eat meat, fish, and beans.

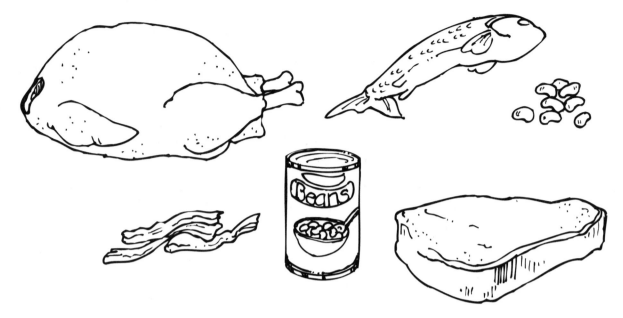

Make a circle around the ones you like best.

5

Learning About My Body • EMC 869

I eat bread, cereal, and grains.

Color the ones you like best.

6

# Rest

## My Body Needs to Rest

• Initiate a discussion about rest and sleep. Ask, "Why is rest important? How do we get rest?" *(nap, sleep)* Explain that rest and sleep give our bodies time to repair themselves and to grow. They allow our bodies to build up energy for the next day.

Read and discuss *Sleep Is for Everyone* by Paul Showers and/or *A Good Night's Sleep* by Allan Fowler.

• Complete a chart entitled "My Body Needs Rest."

My Body Needs Rest
I take a nap.
I sleep at night.
I sit down after I play hard.

page 61

Note: Reproduce this form for each student to use with page 59

Name

Sleep
Early to bed.
Early to rise.
Makes a child
Healthy, happy, and wise.

Draw yourself sleeping in the bed.
Add your favorite stuffed animal or blanket.

I sleep _____ hours every night.

©2000 by Evan-Moor Corp.

• Make the Eager Beaver and Sleepyhead puppets on page 60. Ask students to explain each puppet's name. Discuss how each character might act. Ask students to describe a time when they were "Sleepyheads." Then ask students to explain how getting the right amount of rest helps them to be "Eager Beavers."

• Teach students the verse on page 61. Discuss what the verse tells us to do. Ask students to explain what it means to be "healthy, happy, and wise." Students draw themselves asleep in the bed.

Include this page in each student's logbook.

1.

2.

Sleepyhead

Eager Beaver

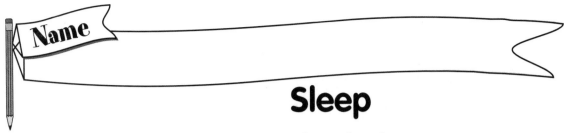

Name

# Sleep

Early to bed.
Early to rise.
Makes a child
Healthy, happy, and wise.

Draw yourself sleeping in the bed.
Add your favorite stuffed animal or blanket.

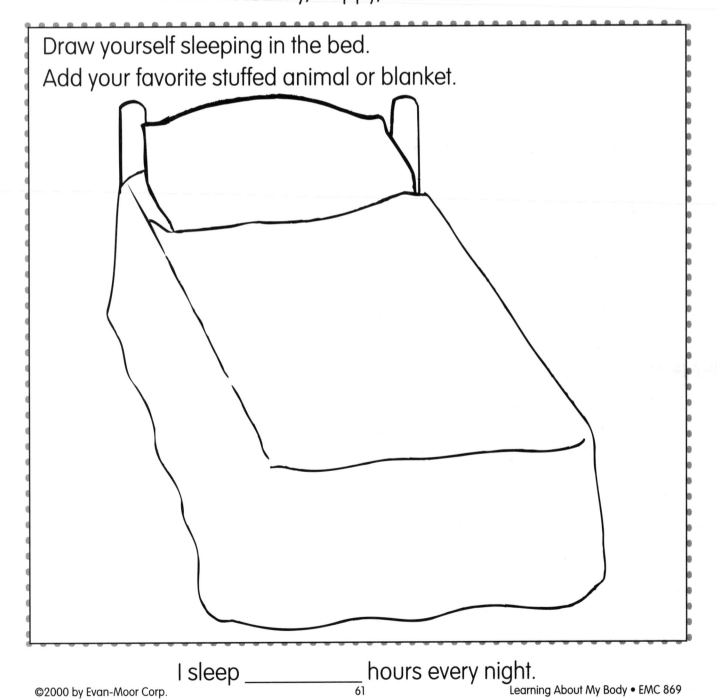

I sleep _____ hours every night.

*Learning About My Body* • EMC 869

# Cleanliness

## I Keep My Body Clean

• Discuss why it is important to be clean. *(So we look clean. So we don't smell. So we don't get sick.)* Ask, "Are there times when it is all right to be dirty?" *(Sometimes when I'm working I get dirty. When I play outside I get dirty.)* Ask, "What do you do to clean yourself up?" *(I take a bath. I wash up. I brush my teeth. I put on clean clothes.)*

Read and discuss *Mortimer Mooner Stopped Taking a Bath* by Frank B. Edwards and appropriate parts of *Good Hygiene* by Alice B. McGinty. Ask students to explain why Mortimer Mooner changed his mind about keeping clean.

• List student responses about why we need to be clean and how we keep clean on a chart entitled "I Keep My Body Clean."

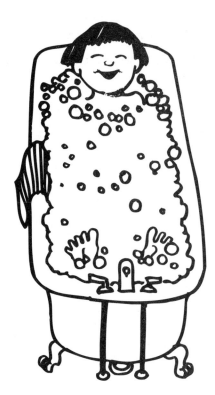

> I Keep My Body Clean
> I wash my hands.
> I take a bath.
> I put on clean clothes.

• Using page 65, students learn a cleanliness rhyme and then paste pictures in the correct boxes as a reminder of what to do each day.

page 65

Learning About My Body • EMC 869

## I Take Care of My Teeth

- Discuss why everyone needs strong teeth. (Guide students to include that teeth help us to eat and speak.) Ask, "What happens if you don't take care of your teeth?" *(Your teeth will look ugly. You will get cavities.)*

  Ask students to describe what they can do to keep their teeth strong and healthy. *(Brush and floss. Don't eat much sugary stuff. Go to the dentist.)* Ask, "Have you ever been to the dentist? What happened there?"

- Write student responses on a chart entitled "We Take Care of Our Teeth."

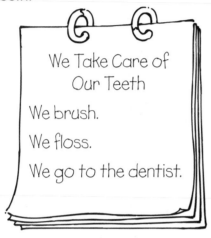

We Take Care of Our Teeth

We brush.

We floss.

We go to the dentist.

- Invite a dentist or dental hygienist to show the class the correct tooth brushing techniques.

- Read and discuss *How Many Teeth?* by Paul Showers, *My Tooth Is About to Fall Out* by Grace MacCarone, or *Andrew's Loose Tooth* by Robert N. Munsch. Then make a "yes/no" graph to show which students have lost a tooth. (See the tooth pattern on page 66.)

- Using page 67, students cut and paste items into categories.

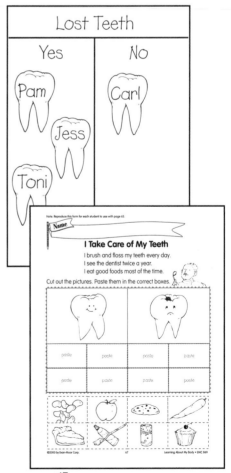

page 67

## Making Connections—Don't Spread Germs

- Explain that some diseases are caused by germs and that germs can be spread from a sick person to a healthy person. There are ways we keep this from happening. Ask students to think of what these ways might be. Use questioning to help them come up with answers. *(Stay away from other people if you are sick. Cover up your mouth when you sneeze. Wash your hands.)*

- Read and discuss appropriate parts of *Germs! Germs! Germs!* by Bobbi Katz and/or *Germs Make Me Sick!* by Melvin Berger.

- Read the minibook on pages 68 and 69. Then model the correct way to wash your hands. Provide time for students to practice the process.

- Do the activity below to remind students to cover up their sneezes and coughs.

---

## Cover Your Sneeze, Please!

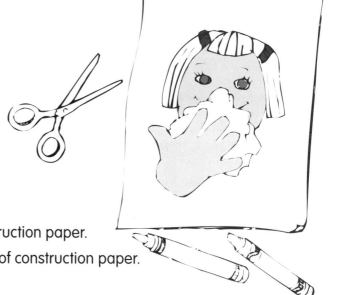

### Materials

- 2 sheets of construction paper— 9" x 12" (23 x 30.5 cm)
- scissors
- crayons
- paste
- tissue

### Steps to Follow

1. Draw your face on one sheet of construction paper.

2. Trace one hand on the second sheet of construction paper.

3. Cut out the hand.

4. Glue the tissue over the mouth and nose. Then glue the hand onto the tissue.

---

 **Logbook**

Include these pages in each student's logbook.

Learning About My Body • EMC 869

Note: Reproduce this form for each student to use with page 62.

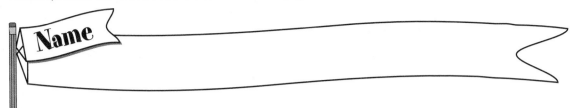

Name

When I go to school each day,
Three things I do with care:

paste

I wash my face.

paste

I brush my teeth.

paste

I always comb my hair.

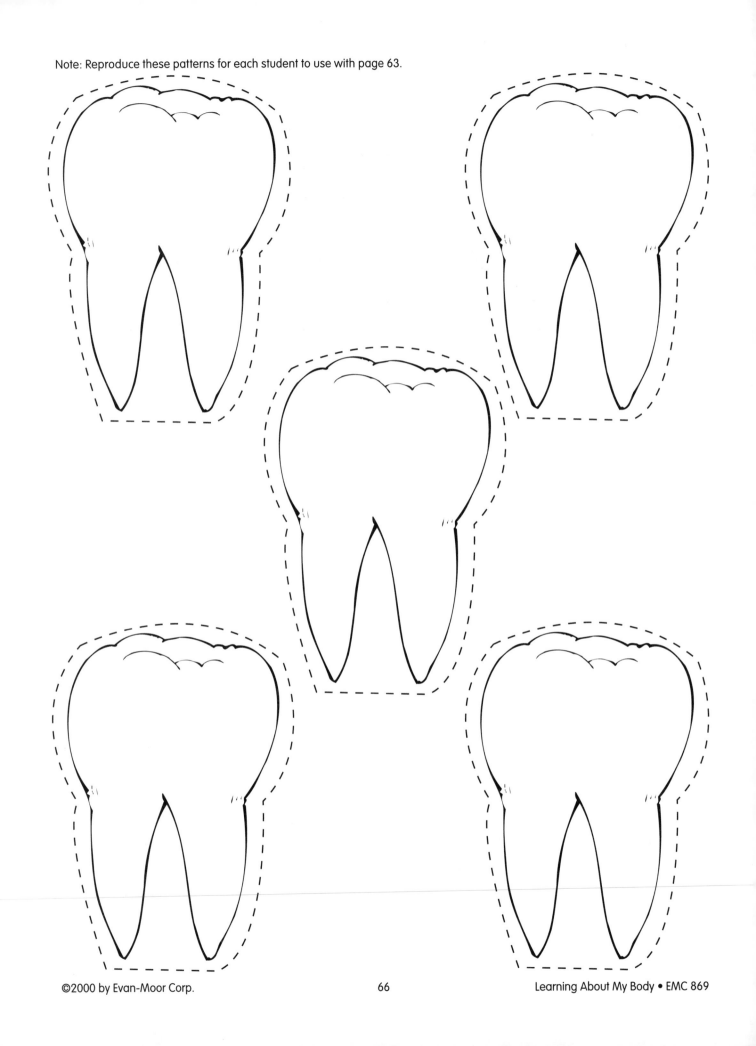

66

Name

# I Take Care of My Teeth

I brush and floss my teeth every day.
I see the dentist twice a year.
I eat good foods most of the time.

Cut out the pictures. Paste them in the correct boxes.

| | |
|---|---|
| paste | paste | paste | paste |
| paste | paste | paste | paste |

# Clean Hands

Wash your hands before you eat.
Dirt from your hands can get on your food.
Wash your hands after going to the bathroom.
Use soap to kill all the germs.

Name:

1

Learning About My Body • EMC 869

**1.** Wet your hands with warm water.
Put soap on your hands.

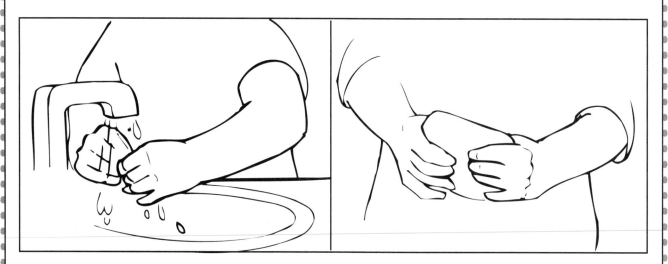

2

Learning About My Body • EMC 869

**2.** Rub your hands together and count to twenty.
The soap bubbles should cover your hands.

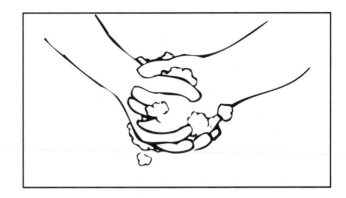

3

**3.** Rinse the soap off under running water. Dry your hands.

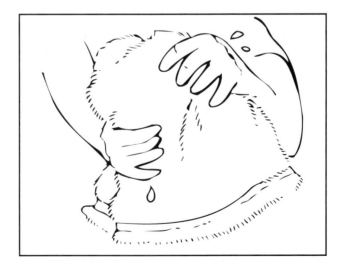

4

# Exercise

## My Body Needs Exercise

- Discuss why exercise is important for a healthy body. *(It keeps us strong.)* Ask students to name ways they get exercise. *(When we do work. When we play. When we run.)*

- List the ways students exercise on a chart entitled "We Get Exercise."

We Get Exercise

We run fast.

We play ball.

We jump rope.

- Take balls and jump ropes outside. Have students demonstrate how they use these tools. Ask them to explain how the exercise helps their bodies. *(My muscles get stronger. My heart beats hard when I jump rope.)*

- Have students draw themselves getting healthy exercise.

- Read and discuss the minibook on pages 71 and 72. Practice the exercises and then send the minibook home to parents.

**My Exercise Book**

My body needs exercise to keep my muscles strong.
I get exercise when I work.
I get exercise when I play.
I can do special exercises, too.

Name:

1

## Logbook

Include this page in each student's logbook.

# My Exercise Book

My body needs exercise to keep my muscles strong.

I get exercise when I work.

I get exercise when I play.

I can do special exercises, too.

**Name:**

1

---

**Toe Touch**

stand tall, feet apart
arms over head

knees bent, bend forward
try to touch your toes

stand up

Do five toe touches at first.

Add more until you can do 20.

2

# Knee Raise

stand tall, feet together
arms down at your sides

back straight, hold right
knee with your hands

pull leg up close
put it down on the floor

Do four knee raises at first.
Add more until you can do 20.

Do the same
thing with your
left knee.

3

Learning About My Body • EMC 869

# Side Leg Raise

lie on your right side
back and legs straight

stretch right arm past your head—use left arm for balance

raise left leg
put it down again

roll over onto left side
raise right leg
put it down again

Start by raising each leg four times.
Work up to raising each leg 30 times.

4

# Safety

## I Try to Be Safe

• Discuss some of the ways bodies can be injured.

*I fell down and skinned my knee.*

*My sister cut her hand with a knife.*

*You can get burned if you play with fire.*

• Read and discuss the minibook on pages 74 and 75.

• Ask students to think of ways they can keep their bodies safe. List ways to be safe on a chart entitled "Safety."

Safety

Wear a helmet when you ride a bike.

Wear a seat belt in the car.

page 76

• Using page 76, students mark the things in the picture that could harm their bodies.

• Make an overhead transparency of page 77 and reproduce a copy for each student. Have students describe the ways the children in the picture are keeping safe and healthy. Then have students mark the healthy children on their copies.

page 77

Include these pages in each student's logbook.

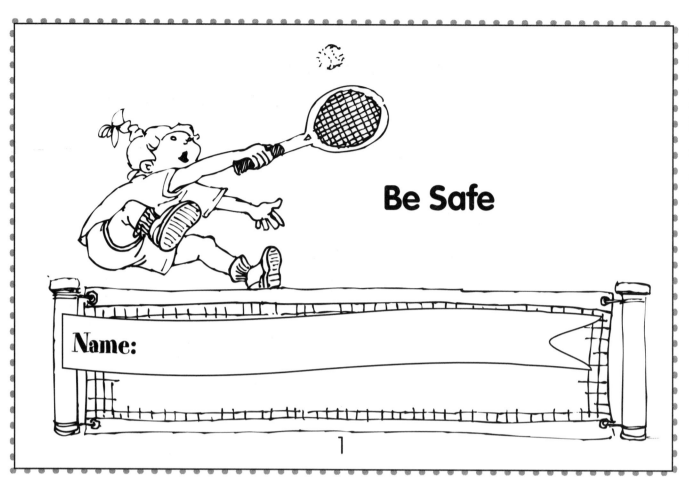

# Be Safe

Name:

1

Wear a bike safety helmet when you ride your bike.
The helmet will protect your head if you fall.

2

Wear a life jacket when you are in a boat.
The life jacket will keep you afloat if you fall into the water.

3

Learning About My Body • EMC 869

Sit down and buckle up when you are in a car.
The seat belt will hold you in your seat if the car stops suddenly.

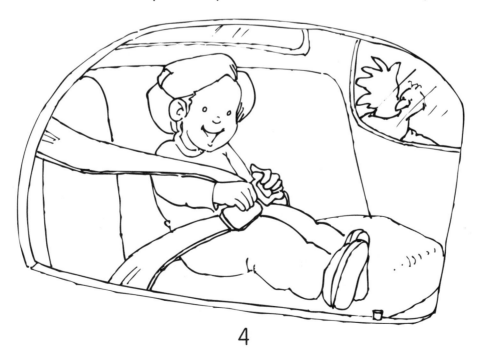

4

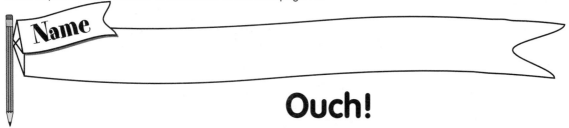

**Name**

# Ouch!

Hot things can burn you.
Sharp things can cut you.
Be careful when you are near
things that can harm your body.

Mark the things in the picture that can harm your body.

# Keeping Healthy Is Fun

Mark the healthy children in this picture.

Tell your family what they are doing to stay healthy.

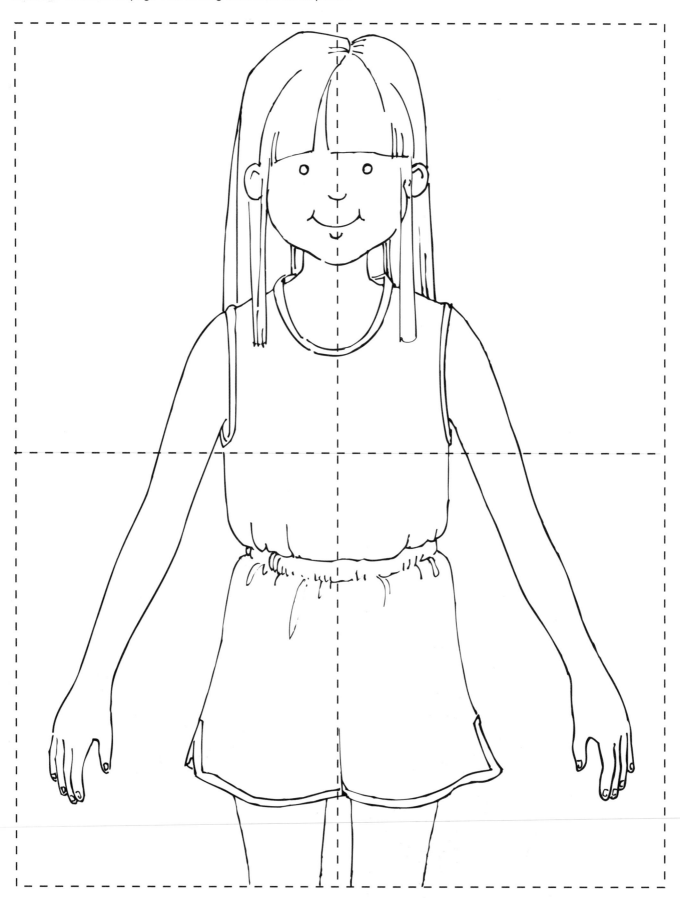

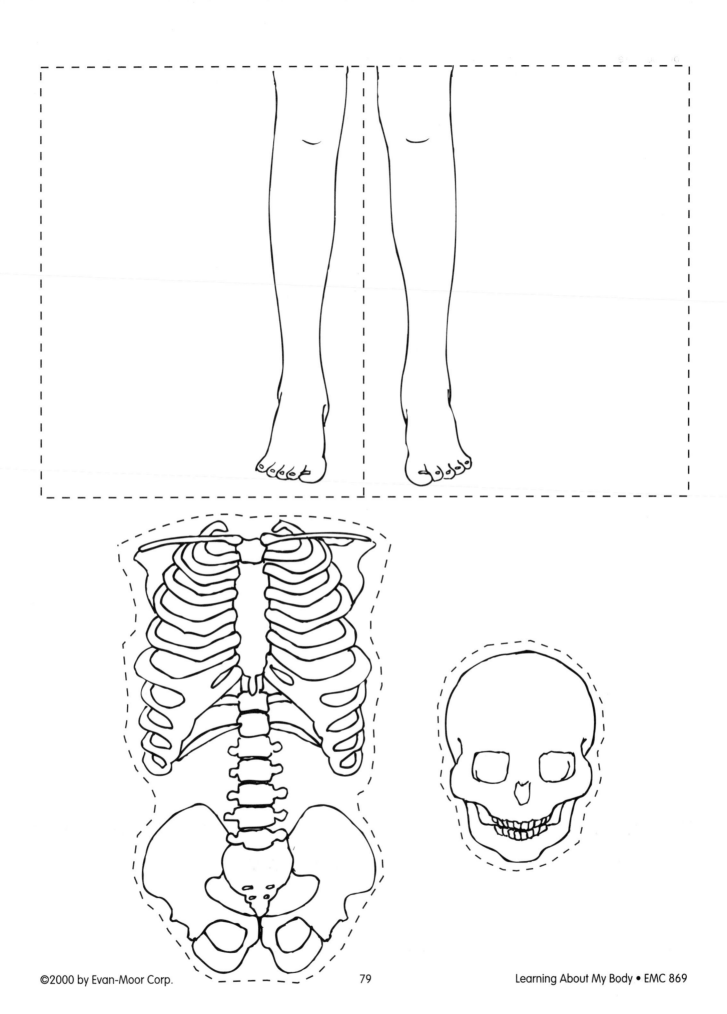

Learning About My Body • EMC 869

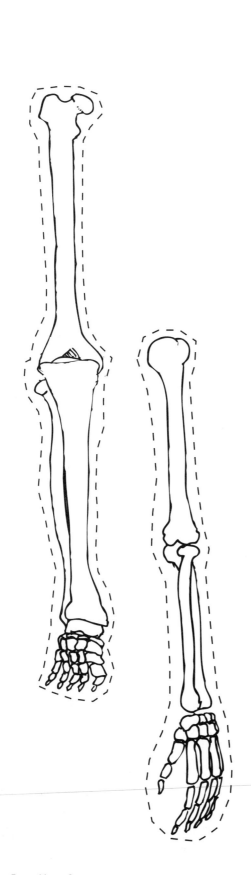

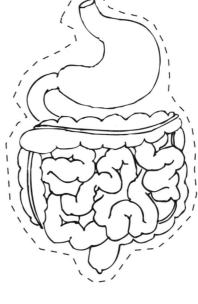

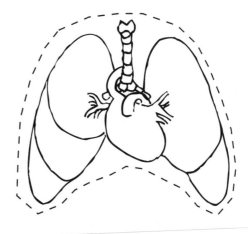

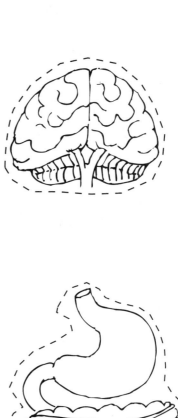

Learning About My Body • EMC 869